MAD LIBS®

By Roger Price and Leonard Stern

PRICE STERN SLOAN
Los Angeles

ISBN: 0-8431-3855-6

1 3 5 7 9 10 8 6 4 2

MAD LIBS®

MAD LIBS® is a game for people who don't like games. It can be played by one, two, three, four, or forty.

■ RIDICULOUSLY SIMPLE DIRECTIONS

In this tablet you will find stories containing blank spaces where words are left out. One player, the **READER**, selects one of these stories. The **READER** does not tell anyone what the story is about. Instead he/she asks the other players, the **WRITERS**, to give him/her words. These words are used to fill in the blank spaces in the story.

■ TO PLAY

The **READER** asks each **WRITER** in turn to call out a word. This word will be an adjective or a noun or whatever the space calls for. He/She then writes the words in the blank spaces in the story. After all the spaces are filled in, the result is a **MAD LIB**.

The **READER** then reads the completed **MAD LIB** to the other players. They will hear that they have written a story that is fantastic, screamingly funny, shocking, silly, crazy, or just plain dumb—depending upon which words each **WRITER** called out.

In case you've forgotten what adjectives, adverbs, nouns, and verbs are, here is a quick review:

An **ADJECTIVE** describes something or somebody. *Lumpy, soft, ugly, messy,* and *short* are adjectives.

An **ADVERB** tells how something is done. It modifies a verb and usually ends in "ly." *Modestly, stupidly, greedily,* and *carefully* are adverbs.

A **NOUN** is the name of a person, place, or thing. *Sidewalk, umbrella, bridle, bathtub,* and *nose* are nouns.

A **VERB** is an action word. *Run, pitch, jump,* and *swim* are verbs.

When we ask for a **GEOGRAPHICAL LOCATION**, we mean any sort of place: a country or city *(Spain, Cleveland)* or a room *(bathroom, kitchen).*

An **EXCLAMATION** or **SILLY WORD** is any sort of funny sound, gasp, grunt, or outcry. *Wow! Ouch! Whomp! Ick!* and *Gadzooks!* are exclamations and silly words.

When we ask for specific words like **A NUMBER, A COLOR, AN ANIMAL,** or **A PART OF THE BODY,** we mean a word that is one of those things.

When a **PLURAL** is asked for, be sure to pluralize the word. For example, *cat* pluralized is *cats.*

EXAMPLE: _____

(BEFORE)

" _____ !" he said
　　　　　　　EXCLAMATION

_____ , as he jumped into his
　　　　　ADVERB

convertible _____ and drove
　　　　　　　　　　　NOUN

off with his _____ wife.
　　　　　　　ADJECTIVE

(AFTER)

" _____*Ouch!*_____ !" he said
　　　　　　　EXCLAMATION

_____*Stupidly*_____ , as he jumped into his
　　　　　ADVERB

convertible _____*cat*_____ and drove
　　　　　　　　　　　NOUN

off with his _____*brave*_____ wife.
　　　　　　　ADJECTIVE

MAD LIBS® is fun to play with friends, but you can also play it by yourself! To begin with, DO NOT look at the story on the page below. Fill in the blanks on this page with the words called for. Then, using the words you've selected, fill in the blank spaces in the story.

Now you've created your own hilarious MAD LIB!

CASPER THE FRIENDLY GHOST

ADJECTIVE: _____

ADJECTIVE: _____

ADJECTIVE: _____

ARTICLE OF CLOTHING:_____

NOUN: _____

ADJECTIVE: _____

ADJECTIVE: _____

PART OF BODY: _____

PLURAL NOUN: _____

ADJECTIVE: _____

NOUN: _____

PLURAL NOUN: _____

VERB: _____

ADVERB: _____

PLURAL NOUN: _____

CASPER THE FRIENDLY GHOST

As most _____ people know, Casper is not
         ADJECTIVE

your average _____ ghost who suddenly
               ADJECTIVE

appears out of _____ air and scares the
                  ADJECTIVE

_____ off of you. Just the opposite,
ARTICLE OF CLOTHING

Casper is as friendly as your next door _____.
                                          NOUN

He always greets you with a/an _____ smile,
                                 ADJECTIVE

a/an _____ handshake, and an encouraging pat
       ADJECTIVE

on your _____. Casper goes out of his way not to
         PART OF BODY

frighten little _____ or even _____
                 PLURAL NOUN   ADJECTIVE

grown-ups. Although Casper has an eerie white _____,
                                                NOUN

he refuses to do other ghostly things such as rattle his

_____ or _____ houses. One learns very
PLURAL NOUN   VERB

_____ that good friends like Casper do not grow on
ADVERB

_____.
PLURAL NOUN

From *Casper*™ *MAD LIBS*® ● Casper © 1995 UCS and Amblin, ™ Harvey
Published by Price Stern Sloan, Inc., a member of The Putnam & Grosset Group, New York, New York.

MAD LIBS® is fun to play with friends, but you can also play it by yourself! To begin with, DO NOT look at the story on the page below. Fill in the blanks on this page with the words called for. Then, using the words you've selected, fill in the blank spaces in the story.

Now you've created your own hilarious MAD LIB!

THE GHOSTLY TRIO

NAME OF PERSON IN ROOM: _____

GEOGRAPHICAL LOCATION: _____

PLURAL NOUN: _____

NOUN: _____

NOUN: _____

NOUN: _____

NOUN: _____

PART OF BODY: _____

SAME NAME OF PERSON IN ROOM: _____

NOUN: _____

EXCLAMATION: _____

ADJECTIVE: _____

SAME NAME OF PERSON IN ROOM: _____

ADJECTIVE: _____

NOUN: _____

SAME NAME OF PERSON IN ROOM: _____

VERB: _____

THE GHOSTLY TRIO

You wouldn't want to meet Casper's uncles, the Ghostly Trio—Stretch,

Stinkie, and Fatso, otherwise known as _____
NAME OF PERSON IN ROOM

—in a dark _____ . They love to haunt and
GEOGRAPHICAL LOCATION

taunt human _____ . Stretch, the leader, is a
PLURAL NOUN

bully and a _____ . Stinkie lives up to his name. He's the
NOUN

meanest _____ in the spirit world, and he smells worse
NOUN

than Roquefort _____ . Stinkie loves to morph from one
NOUN

character to another _____ and frighten humans out of
NOUN

their _____ . _____
PART OF BODY   SAME NAME OF PERSON IN ROOM

can eat you out of house and _____ in less time than it
NOUN

takes to say _____ ! Although happy-go-lucky and
EXCLAMATION

_____-natured, _____
ADJECTIVE   SAME NAME OF PERSON IN ROOM

has a/an _____ temper and can fly off
ADJECTIVE

the _____ without warning. Beware! . . .
NOUN

_____ has been known to sit on
SAME NAME OF PERSON IN ROOM

humans and _____ them to death.
VERB

From *Casper™ MAD LIBS* ® ● Casper © 1995 UCS and Amblin, ™ Harvey
Published by Price Stern Sloan, Inc., a member of The Putnam & Grosset Group, New York, New York.

MAD LIBS® is fun to play with friends, but you can also play it by yourself! To begin with, DO NOT look at the story on the page below. Fill in the blanks on this page with the words called for. Then, using the words you've selected, fill in the blank spaces in the story.

Now you've created your own hilarious MAD LIB!

ALL YOU NEED TO KNOW ABOUT CASPER

NOUN:_____

NAME OF PERSON: _____

PLURAL NOUN: _____

PLURAL NOUN: _____

NOUN:_____

NOUN:_____

NOUN:_____

ADJECTIVE: _____

NOUN:_____

ADJECTIVE: _____

ADJECTIVE: _____

PLURAL NOUN: _____

NOUN:_____

ARTICLE OF CLOTHING:_____

LETTER:_____

LETTER:_____

NUMBER:_____

ALL YOU NEED TO KNOW ABOUT CASPER

Casper first saw the light of _____ as a cartoon in a
                                              NOUN

magazine called _____ . He became one
                            NAME OF PERSON

of the most popular _____ in newspapers
                                  PLURAL NOUN

throughout our United _____ before becoming a
                              PLURAL NOUN

favorite Saturday morning television _____. Casper is
                                         NOUN

now the star of a major motion _____ that you can see
                                  NOUN

in your local _____. The Casper movie is a/an
                      NOUN

_____ blend of _____ -generated
    ADJECTIVE   NOUN

animation and _____ live action. It's _____
                ADJECTIVE   ADJECTIVE

fun and exciting! The movie has enough scary _____
                                      PLURAL NOUN

to keep you on the edge of your _____ and frighten the
                                   NOUN

_____ off of you. Warning: Casper is rated
    ARTICLE OF CLOTHING

_____ _____ - _____ .
 LETTER   LETTER   NUMBER

From Casper™ MAD LIBS® ● Casper © 1995 UCS and Amblin, ™ Harvey
Published by Price Stern Sloan, Inc., a member of The Putnam & Grosset Group, New York, New York.

MAD LIBS® is fun to play with friends, but you can also play it by yourself! To begin with, DO NOT look at the story on the page below. Fill in the blanks on this page with the words called for. Then, using the words you've selected, fill in the blank spaces in the story.

Now you've created your own hilarious MAD LIB!

CASPER THE MOVIE, PART 1

PLURAL NOUN: _____

ADVERB: _____

PLURAL NOUN: _____

NICKNAME (PLURAL): _____

NOUN: _____

ADJECTIVE: _____

ADJECTIVE: _____

ADJECTIVE: _____

VERB (PAST TENSE): _____

ADJECTIVE: _____

ADVERB: _____

PART OF BODY: _____

PLURAL NOUN: _____

PLURAL NOUN: _____

ADJECTIVE: _____

NOUN: _____

CASPER THE MOVIE, PART 1

For many years, the supernatural _____ of
                                       PLURAL NOUN

Whipstaff Manor have guarded their home _____.
                                                ADVERB

These ghosts wouldn't allow any human _____,
                                            PLURAL NOUN

whom they nicknamed _____ , to step across
                         NICKNAME (PLURAL)

their _____ . Unfortunately, this left Casper a very
           NOUN

_____ ghost without any _____
    ADJECTIVE   ADJECTIVE

friends. When Casper learned that the _____
                                            ADJECTIVE

owner of Whipstaff had _____ away and the
                          VERB (PAST TENSE)

manor had been inherited by his _____
                                       ADJECTIVE

daughter, Carrigan, he greeted this news _____ .
                                              ADVERB

"Wow!" he shouted at the top of his _____ .
                                        PART OF BODY

"Now I'll have a friend to share my most intimate

_____ with! And we'll play all kinds of
     PLURAL NOUN

_____ ." Will this _____
     PLURAL NOUN   ADJECTIVE

dream of Casper's come true? To be continued on Casper the

_____ , Part 2.
      NOUN

MAD LIBS® is fun to play with friends, but you can also play it by yourself! To begin with, DO NOT look at the story on the page below. Fill in the blanks on this page with the words called for. Then, using the words you've selected, fill in the blank spaces in the story.

Now you've created your own hilarious MAD LIB!

CHRISTMAS GHOSTS

PLURAL NOUN: _____

ADJECTIVE: _____

NOUN: _____

PART OF BODY: _____

PLURAL NOUN: _____

ADJECTIVE: _____

VERB (ENDING IN "S"): _____

ADJECTIVE: _____

NOUN: _____

ADJECTIVE: _____

NOUN: _____

PART OF BODY: _____

NOUN: _____

ADJECTIVE: _____

ADJECTIVE: _____

NOUN: _____

NOUN: _____

CHRISTMAS GHOSTS

Four of Casper's favorite _____ are the ghosts
PLURAL NOUN

in Charles Dickens' _____ tale, *A Christmas Carol*.
ADJECTIVE

This story has become as much a part of Christmas tradition as the

holly _____ , mistle-_____ , and
NOUN   PART OF BODY

Christmas _____ . *A Christmas Carol* tells the
PLURAL NOUN

story of Ebenezer Scrooge, a/an _____ miser who
ADJECTIVE

_____ pennies! It isn't until Scrooge meets
VERB (ENDING IN "S")

up with the ghost of his dead and _____ partner,
ADJECTIVE

Jacob Marley, and the ghost of Christmas past, that he learns

what a terrible _____ he has been all of his
NOUN

_____ life. Through these ghosts, Scrooge learns
ADJECTIVE

to be a generous _____ and to honor the spirit of
NOUN

Christmas in his _____ . Mending his ways, Scrooge
PART OF BODY

sends a Christmas _____ to his _____
NOUN   ADJECTIVE

clerk, Bob Cratchett, and Bob's son _____ Tim. He
ADJECTIVE

also donates large sums of _____ to the poor and finally
NOUN

shows up at the door of his nephew's house for Christmas

_____ .
NOUN

From *Casper™ MAD LIBS®* ● Casper © 1995 UCS and Amblin, ™ Harvey
Published by Price Stern Sloan, Inc., a member of The Putnam & Grosset Group, New York, New York.

MAD LIBS® is fun to play with friends, but you can also play it by yourself! To begin with, DO NOT look at the story on the page below. Fill in the blanks on this page with the words called for. Then, using the words you've selected, fill in the blank spaces in the story.

Now you've created your own hilarious MAD LIB!

CARRIGAN CRITTENDEN, NOT A VERY NICE PERSON

PLURAL NOUN: _____

ADJECTIVE: _____

PLURAL NOUN: _____

ADJECTIVE: _____

PART OF BODY: _____

NOUN: _____

NOUN: _____

ADJECTIVE: _____

ADJECTIVE: _____

PLURAL NOUN: _____

VERB (ENDING IN "S"): _____

PART OF BODY (PLURAL): _____

ADJECTIVE: _____

PLURAL NOUN: _____

CARRIGAN CRITTENDEN, NOT A VERY NICE PERSON

One of the leading _____ in the movie *Casper* is

PLURAL NOUN

Carrigan Crittenden. Carrigan is a wicked and _____

ADJECTIVE

woman who always dresses in black _____ and

PLURAL NOUN

wears _____ glasses to cover her _____ .

ADJECTIVE · PART OF BODY

Hardly anyone has a kind _____ for her. At the reading

NOUN

of her father's _____ , Carrigan learns all she has

NOUN

inherited is his _____ mansion. His fortune has

ADJECTIVE

been left to other _____ relatives and charitable

ADJECTIVE

_____ . Infuriated, Carrigan _____

PLURAL NOUN · VERB (ENDING IN "S")

at the top of her _____ , vowing to get

PART OF BODY (PLURAL)

even with her _____ father and any other

ADJECTIVE

_____ that stand in her way.

PLURAL NOUN

From *Casper™ MAD LIBS®* ● Casper © 1995 UCS and Amblin, ™ Harvey
Published by Price Stern Sloan, Inc., a member of The Putnam & Grosset Group, New York, New York.

MAD LIBS® is fun to play with friends, but you can also play it by yourself! To begin with, DO NOT look at the story on the page below. Fill in the blanks on this page with the words called for. Then, using the words you've selected, fill in the blank spaces in the story.

Now you've created your own hilarious MAD LIB!

LOOKING FOR A BUDDY

ADJECTIVE: _____

PLURAL NOUN: _____

PLURAL NOUN: _____

PLURAL NOUN: _____

PLURAL NOUN: _____

PLURAL NOUN: _____

PLURAL NOUN: _____

ADJECTIVE: _____

NOUN: _____

NOUN: _____

NOUN: _____

LOOKING FOR A BUDDY

Casper has been waiting with _____ patience for
ADJECTIVE

someone special to walk through the _____ of
PLURAL NOUN

Whipstaff Manor. He needs a friend with whom he can share his

innermost _____, someone to whom he can tell his
PLURAL NOUN

deepest, darkest _____, and most of all someone
PLURAL NOUN

with whom he can play games such as _____
PLURAL NOUN

and _____. When Kat shows up at Whipstaff
PLURAL NOUN

Manor, Casper knows in his heart of _____ that
PLURAL NOUN

they are destined to be _____ friends. Kat, though,
ADJECTIVE

is not so sure that Casper will be her soul _____.
NOUN

Later on, even though Casper is a ghost and Kat is a real live

_____, they become as close as two peas in
NOUN

a/an _____.
NOUN

From *Casper™ MAD LIBS* ® ● Casper © 1995 UCS and Amblin, ™ Harvey
Published by Price Stern Sloan, Inc., a member of The Putnam & Grosset Group, New York, New York.

MAD LIBS® is fun to play with friends, but you can also play it by yourself! To begin with, DO NOT look at the story on the page below. Fill in the blanks on this page with the words called for. Then, using the words you've selected, fill in the blank spaces in the story.

Now you've created your own hilarious MAD LIB!

CASPER THE MOVIE, PART 2

ADJECTIVE: _____

NOUN: _____

PLURAL NOUN: _____

SAME PLURAL NOUN: _____

ADJECTIVE: _____

NOUN: _____

ADJECTIVE: _____

PART OF BODY (PLURAL): _____

ADJECTIVE: _____

NOUN: _____

NOUN: _____

NOUN: _____

NUMBER: _____

VERB (PAST TENSE): _____

CASPER THE MOVIE, PART 2

When Carrigan and her _____ partner, Dibs, arrive
                        ADJECTIVE

at Whipstaff Manor, they count on finding Casper's hidden

_____. What they don't count on are Casper's
      NOUN

uncles, Stretch, Stinkie, and Fatso, known as the Ghostly

_____. Unable to cope with the Ghostly
   PLURAL NOUN

_____, Carrigan sends for the _____
  SAME PLURAL NOUN   ADJECTIVE

Dr. Harvey, who is known as the greatest _____ in
                                              NOUN

the whole _____ world. Dr. Harvey has his
            ADJECTIVE

_____ full dealing with the Ghostly
  PART OF BODY (PLURAL)

Trio. But fate presents Carrigan with a/an _____
                                                ADJECTIVE

opportunity. Learning there may be a/an _____
                                             NOUN

buried at Whipstaff, she jumps into her _____,
                                             NOUN

accelerates the _____, and drives off at _____
                    NOUN   NUMBER

miles an hour. Will she find the fortune?

To be _____ in Casper the Movie, Part 3.
        VERB (PAST TENSE)

From Casper™ MAD LIBS® ● Casper © 1995 UCS and Amblin, ™ Harvey
Published by Price Stern Sloan, Inc., a member of The Putnam & Grosset Group, New York, New York.

MAD LIBS® is fun to play with friends, but you can also play it by yourself! To begin with, DO NOT look at the story on the page below. Fill in the blanks on this page with the words called for. Then, using the words you've selected, fill in the blank spaces in the story.

Now you've created your own hilarious MAD LIB!

MEET KAT HARVEY

ADJECTIVE: _____

NOUN: _____

PLURAL NOUN: _____

NUMBER: _____

GEOGRAPHICAL LOCATION (PLURAL): _____

NUMBER: _____

PLURAL NOUN: _____

PART OF BODY: _____

PART OF BODY: _____

NOUN: _____

VERB: _____

ADJECTIVE: _____

PART OF BODY: _____

ADJECTIVE: _____

MEET KAT HARVEY

Having moved with her father from one city to another for most of

her _____ life, Kat Harvey has never been in the
          ADJECTIVE

same _____ long enough to make friends with any
              NOUN

_____ her own age. All told, in her brief
      PLURAL NOUN

lifetime, Kat has lived in _____ different
                                      NUMBER

_____ , attended as many as
      GEOGRAPHICAL LOCATION (PLURAL)

_____ public _____ , and has had
      NUMBER   PLURAL NOUN

more teachers than you can shake a _____ at.
                                          PART OF BODY

Enjoying Casper and Whipstaff Manor, Kat decides to put her

_____ down and tell Dr. Harvey in a heart-to-
      PART OF BODY

_____ talk that she doesn't want to _____
      NOUN   VERB

anymore. To her _____ surprise, Dr. Harvey agrees
                        ADJECTIVE

with her. He pats her fondly on her _____ and
                                          PART OF BODY

says, "The next time we move, it is going to be over my

_____ body."
      ADJECTIVE

From *Casper™ MAD LIBS* ® ● Casper © 1995 UCS and Amblin, ™ Harvey

Published by Price Stern Sloan, Inc., a member of The Putnam & Grosset Group, New York, New York.

MAD LIBS® is fun to play with friends, but you can also play it by yourself! To begin with, DO NOT look at the story on the page below. Fill in the blanks on this page with the words called for. Then, using the words you've selected, fill in the blank spaces in the story.

Now you've created your own hilarious MAD LIB!

THREE OF CASPER'S FAVORITE THINGS TO DO

VERB: _____

ADJECTIVE: _____

PLURAL NOUN: _____

PLURAL NOUN: _____

NOUN: _____

PART OF BODY (PLURAL): _____

PART OF BODY: _____

VERB: _____

NOUN: _____

NOUN: _____

LAST NAME OF PERSON (PLURAL): _____

ADJECTIVE: _____

VERB (ENDING IN "ING"): _____

ADJECTIVE: _____

NOUN: _____

NOUN: _____

PLURAL NOUN: _____

PLURAL NOUN: _____

THREE OF CASPER'S FAVORITE THINGS TO DO

Casper loves to _____ with nature. Almost every day, he
     VERB

takes _____ walks in the woods, always stopping to
  ADJECTIVE

smell the _____ , and feeds the_____ .
  PLURAL NOUN   PLURAL NOUN

Music makes Casper one happy _____ . He can't stop
         NOUN

drumming his _____ or tapping his
    PART OF BODY (PLURAL)

_____ when he plays rock and _____
 PART OF BODY   VERB

on his four-speaker _____ . Casper's all-time
      NOUN

favorite _____ performers are the "Dead
   NOUN

_____" and "The
LAST NAME OF PERSON IN ROOM (PLURAL)

_____ Dead." Probably nothing gives Casper more
 ADJECTIVE

pleasure than _____ a/an _____
    VERB (ENDING IN "ING")   ADJECTIVE

book. Someday he hopes to have a library filled with floor-to-

_____ bookcases made of _____ and
 NOUN   NOUN

packed with books about great baseball _____
           PLURAL NOUN

and famous dead _____ .
    PLURAL NOUN

From Casper™ MAD LIBS® ● Casper © 1995 UCS and Amblin, ™ Harvey
Published by Price Stern Sloan, Inc., a member of The Putnam & Grosset Group, New York, New York.

MAD LIBS® is fun to play with friends, but you can also play it by yourself! To begin with, DO NOT look at the story on the page below. Fill in the blanks on this page with the words called for. Then, using the words you've selected, fill in the blank spaces in the story.

Now you've created your own hilarious MAD LIB!

A GHOST OF A CHANCE

PART OF BODY (PLURAL): _____

PART OF BODY: _____

VERB (ENDING IN "ING"): _____

NOUN: _____

PART OF BODY: _____

PART OF BODY: _____

COLOR: _____

NOUN: _____

PART OF BODY: _____

COLOR: _____

PART OF BODY: _____

ADJECTIVE: _____

ADJECTIVE: _____

ADJECTIVE: _____

NUMBER: _____

A GHOST OF A CHANCE

When Casper first saw Kat Harvey, he couldn't believe his

_____. His _____
  PART OF BODY (PLURAL)   PART OF BODY

started thumping, his knees started _____,
                                         VERB (ENDING IN "ING")

and he couldn't even remember his own _____.
                                                 NOUN

When he looked her over from _____ to
                                       PART OF BODY

_____, he saw that she had _____
        PART OF BODY   COLOR

shoulder-length _____ that fell gently on her
                         NOUN

_____ and her eyes were a sparkling
        PART OF BODY

_____. Best of all, Casper thought, were the
        COLOR

delightful little dimples on both sides of her lovely

_____. When he got to know Kat, Casper
        PART OF BODY

was equally impressed with her _____ mind, her
                                        ADJECTIVE

_____ vocabulary, and most of all, her
        ADJECTIVE

_____ sense of humor. This girl was one in
        ADJECTIVE

_____!
        NUMBER

From Casper™ MAD LIBS® ● Casper © 1995 UCS and Amblin, ™ Harvey
Published by Price Stern Sloan, Inc., a member of The Putnam & Grosset Group, New York, New York.

MAD LIBS® is fun to play with friends, but you can also play it by yourself! To begin with, DO NOT look at the story on the page below. Fill in the blanks on this page with the words called for. Then, using the words you've selected, fill in the blank spaces in the story.

Now you've created your own hilarious MAD LIB!

FOOD FOR THOUGHT

PART OF BODY (PLURAL): _____

NOUN: _____

ADJECTIVE: _____

ADJECTIVE: _____

NOUN: _____

PLURAL NOUN: _____

VERB (PAST TENSE): _____

NUMBER: _____

NOUN: _____

PLURAL NOUN: _____

NOUN: _____

NOUN: _____

ADJECTIVE: _____

PLURAL NOUN: _____

NOUN: _____

NOUN: _____

PLURAL NOUN: _____

PLURAL NOUN: _____

FOOD FOR THOUGHT

Ghosts can eat to their _____ content without
PART OF BODY (PLURAL)

ever putting on a single _____. Here's a list of Uncle
NOUN

Fatso's five _____ foods:
ADJECTIVE

1. A/an _____ hamburger on a toasted _____
   ADJECTIVE NOUN

   with a side of french-fried _____.
   PLURAL NOUN

2. Seven _____ eggs with _____
   VERB (PAST TENSE) NUMBER

   strips of _____ and a stack of _____
   NOUN PLURAL NOUN

   covered with maple syrup.

3. Tacos filled with _____, lettuce, and _____.
   NOUN NOUN

4. A thick, _____ T-bone steak smothered with
   ADJECTIVE

   _____ and served with a baked _____.
   PLURAL NOUN NOUN

5. And of course, junk food! A big bag of _____ chips,
   NOUN

   fresh roasted _____, and chocolate-filled
   PLURAL NOUN

   _____.
   PLURAL NOUN

MAD LIBS® is fun to play with friends, but you can also play it by yourself! To begin with, DO NOT look at the story on the page below. Fill in the blanks on this page with the words called for. Then, using the words you've selected, fill in the blank spaces in the story.

Now you've created your own hilarious MAD LIB!

FRANKENSTEIN

VERB: _____

ADJECTIVE: _____

NOUN: _____

NOUN: _____

ADJECTIVE: _____

ADVERB (ENDING IN "LY"): _____

ADJECTIVE: _____

NOUN: _____

NAME OF PERSON IN ROOM: _____

NOUN: _____

ADVERB (ENDING IN "LY"): _____

PART OF BODY (PLURAL): _____

PLURAL NOUN: _____

SAME NAME OF PERSON IN ROOM: _____

PLURAL NOUN: _____

ADJECTIVE: _____

ADJECTIVE: _____

SAME NAME OF PERSON IN ROOM: _____

PLURAL NOUN: _____

FRANKENSTEIN

One of Casper's favorite books to _____ is Mary
                                        VERB

Shelley's *Frankenstein*. It is the _____ story of a
                                        ADJECTIVE

doctor who lives in a gloomy old _____ on the top of a
                                      NOUN

high _____ . Dr. Frankenstein has a/an _____
        NOUN   ADJECTIVE

laboratory in his basement in which he is _____
                                          ADVERB (ENDING IN "LY")

trying to create a/an _____ monster, but
                          ADJECTIVE

unfortunately, ends up with a/an _____ that looks like
                                      NOUN

_____ . When the townspeople learn of
  NAME OF PERSON IN ROOM

the _____ , they gather and demand it be destroyed
        NOUN

_____ . The doctor refuses. The townspeople.
  ADVERB (ENDING IN "LY")

decide to take matters into their own _____ .
                                      PART OF BODY (PLURAL)

They go after the monster, hurling sticks and _____ at
                                                  PLURAL NOUN

_____ . Feeling bewildered and
  SAME NAME OF PERSON IN ROOM

betrayed, the monster starts to sob and _____
                                          PLURAL NOUN

roll down its _____ face. More fearful of the people
                  ADJECTIVE

than they are of it, the _____ monster runs away!
                              ADJECTIVE

_____ is never heard from or
  SAME NAME OF PERSON IN ROOM

seen again until becoming a famous star in major motion

_____ in Hollywood.
  PLURAL NOUN

From *Casper™ MAD LIBS* ® ● Casper © 1995 UCS and Amblin, ™ Harvey
Published by Price Stern Sloan, Inc., a member of The Putnam & Grosset Group, New York, New York.

MAD LIBS® is fun to play with friends, but you can also play it by yourself! To begin with, DO NOT look at the story on the page below. Fill in the blanks on this page with the words called for. Then, using the words you've selected, fill in the blank spaces in the story.

Now you've created your own hilarious MAD LIB!

BEST OF BEST FRIENDS

ADJECTIVE: _____

ADVERB: _____

PART OF BODY: _____

ADJECTIVE: _____

PART OF BODY: _____

ADJECTIVE: _____

PLURAL NOUN: _____

PART OF BODY: _____

NOUN: _____

PLURAL NOUN: _____

ADVERB (ENDING IN "LY"): _____

PART OF BODY: _____

NOUN: _____

VERB: _____

ADVERB: _____

PART OF BODY: _____

COLOR: _____

BEST OF BEST FRIENDS

"It's fun to have a/an _____ friend like you,
                            ADJECTIVE

Casper," says Kat, patting Casper _____ on his
                                          ADVERB

_____.
PART OF BODY

"Thanks!" replies Casper, a/an _____ smile lighting
                                      ADJECTIVE

up his _____.
        PART OF BODY

"We're truly lucky," adds Kat, "most ordinary people can count the

number of _____ friends they have on the five
                  ADJECTIVE

_____ of their _____."
PLURAL NOUN   PART OF BODY

"True," says Casper, "I knew the first _____ I saw you
                                              NOUN

that we were going to be best _____."
                                    PLURAL NOUN

"I felt that, too," says Kat _____.
                              ADVERB (ENDING IN "LY")

"Would you put your _____ on a _____
                        PART OF BODY   NOUN

and swear we will be friends as long as we _____?"
                                                  VERB

Casper says he would _____. The two friends walk
                            ADVERB

off hand in _____ into the _____
              PART OF BODY   COLOR

sunset.

From *Casper*™ *MAD LIBS* ® ● Casper © 1995 UCS and Amblin, ™ Harvey
Published by Price Stern Sloan, Inc., a member of The Putnam & Grosset Group, New York, New York.

MAD LIBS® is fun to play with friends, but you can also play it by yourself! To begin with, DO NOT look at the story on the page below. Fill in the blanks on this page with the words called for. Then, using the words you've selected, fill in the blank spaces in the story.

Now you've created your own hilarious MAD LIB!

THE LEGEND OF SLEEPY HOLLOW

NOUN: _____

PLURAL NOUN: _____

ADJECTIVE: _____

NOUN: _____

ADJECTIVE: _____

PART OF THE BODY (PLURAL): _____

ADJECTIVE: _____

NOUN: _____

ADJECTIVE: _____

ADJECTIVE: _____

PART OF BODY: _____

ADJECTIVE: _____

PLURAL NOUN: _____

NOUN: _____

PART OF BODY: _____

THE LEGEND OF SLEEPY HOLLOW

Casper loves scary _____ stories, especially those
                          NOUN

that give him goose _____. One of his favorites
                        PLURAL NOUN

is Washington Irving's _____ tale, *The Legend of*
                              ADJECTIVE

Sleepy _____. This is a story about Ichabod Crane,
                NOUN

a/an _____ school teacher who because of his long
          ADJECTIVE

_____ looks like a/an _____
PART OF BODY (PLURAL)   ADJECTIVE

scarecrow. Ichabod believes in ghosts, especially the Headless

_____ of Sleepy Hollow. One dark and _____
          NOUN   ADJECTIVE

night, coming home from a party astride his _____
                                                      ADJECTIVE

horse, Ichabod sees something off in the distance that makes his

_____ stand on end. It is the _____
    PART OF BODY   ADJECTIVE

Horseman! Scared out of his _____, Ichabod spurs
                                    PLURAL NOUN

his _____ into a gallop and disappears into the woods.
          NOUN

Neither hide nor _____ of Ichabod is ever seen
                        PART OF BODY

again.

From *Casper*™ *MAD LIBS* ® ● Casper © 1995 UCS and Amblin, ™ Harvey
Published by Price Stern Sloan, Inc., a member of The Putnam & Grosset Group, New York, New York.

MAD LIBS® is fun to play with friends, but you can also play it by yourself! To begin with, DO NOT look at the story on the page below. Fill in the blanks on this page with the words called for. Then, using the words you've selected, fill in the blank spaces in the story.

Now you've created your own hilarious MAD LIB!

NO THANKS FOR THE PRANKS

EXCLAMATION: _____

VERB (PAST TENSE): _____

PLURAL NOUN: _____

ADJECTIVE: _____

NOUN: _____

PART OF BODY: _____

ADJECTIVE: _____

ADJECTIVE: _____

PART OF BODY: _____

ADJECTIVE: _____

ANIMAL: _____

ADJECTIVE: _____

ADVERB: _____

PART OF BODY: _____

PART OF BODY: _____

ADVERB (ENDING IN "LY"): _____

PART OF BODY: _____

NO THANKS FOR THE PRANKS

"_____!" Kat shouted as Casper
　　　　EXCLAMATION

_____ through the wall into the room. Soon,
　VERB (PAST TENSE)

hundreds of antique _____ were moving about to
　　　　　　　　　　PLURAL NOUN

_____ music. "What are you doing?" asked Kat.
ADJECTIVE

"I'm just having fun," said Casper. "If you don't want me around, I

can disappear into thin _____ or make myself invisible
　　　　　　　　　　NOUN

to the naked _____."
　　　　PART OF BODY

"No," answered Kat. "Just give me a _____ warning
　　　　　　　　　　　　　　　ADJECTIVE

when you are going to play one of your _____
　　　　　　　　　　　　　　　　　　　ADJECTIVE

pranks."

This worried Casper. "You don't have a weak _____,
　　　　　　　　　　　　　　　　　　　PART OF BODY

do you?" he asked with _____ concern.
　　　　　　　　ADJECTIVE

"No," replied Kat. "I'm as strong as a/an _____, but
　　　　　　　　　　　　　　　　　　ANIMAL

I don't appreciate your _____ antics."
　　　　　　　　　ADJECTIVE

"I won't do them anymore," promised Casper _____.
　　　　　　　　　　　　　　　　　ADVERB

As a gesture of friendship, he held out his _____.
　　　　　　　　　　　　　　　　PART OF BODY

Kat shook his _____ _____ and
　　　　　PART OF BODY　　ADVERB (ENDING IN "LY")

gave him a kiss on the side of his _____.
　　　　　　　　　　　　　　PART OF BODY

From *Casper™ MAD LIBS* ® ● Casper © 1995 UCS and Amblin, ™ Harvey
Published by Price Stern Sloan, Inc., a member of The Putnam & Grosset Group, New York, New York.

MAD LIBS® is fun to play with friends, but you can also play it by yourself! To begin with, DO NOT look at the story on the page below. Fill in the blanks on this page with the words called for. Then, using the words you've selected, fill in the blank spaces in the story.

Now you've created your own hilarious MAD LIB!

CASPER THE MOVIE, PART 3

NOUN: _____

LIQUID: _____

NOUN: _____

VERB (ENDING IN "S"): _____

ADJECTIVE: _____

PLURAL NOUN: _____

PART OF BODY: _____

SAME LIQUID: _____

NOUN: _____

ADVERB: _____

ADJECTIVE: _____

NOUN: _____

ADJECTIVE: _____

VERB: _____

ADJECTIVE: _____

PLURAL NOUN: _____

CASPER THE MOVIE, PART 3

Carrigan trails Casper and Kat down into the _____
NOUN

of Whipstaff where she discovers a vial of magical

_____ that can turn a human _____ into a
LIQUID   NOUN

ghost and vice-versa. Carrigan _____ the
                        VERB (ENDING IN "S")

contents of the magical vial. As a ghost, she is outraged to discover

Casper's _____ treasure is nothing more than a few of
         ADJECTIVE

his favorite _____. She looks for Casper to wring his
             PLURAL NOUN

_____ . Casper, about to drink the _____
PART OF BODY   SAME LIQUID

from the vial and change himself back into a little _____,
                                                     NOUN

sees Kat's dad, Dr. Harvey, who has become a ghost himself.

_____ , Casper realizes that there is only enough
ADVERB

_____ liquid left to bring either him or Dr. Harvey
ADJECTIVE

back from the _____. In an act of _____
              NOUN   ADJECTIVE

courage, Casper sacrifices himself so that Dr. Harvey can

_____ again. Don't despair, our story has a
VERB

_____ ending. Casper and Kat finally become best
ADJECTIVE

_____ for life and afterlife.
PLURAL NOUN

From *Casper*™ *MAD LIBS*® ● Casper © 1995 UCS and Amblin, ™ Harvey
Published by Price Stern Sloan, Inc., a member of The Putnam & Grosset Group, New York, New York.

MAD LIBS® is fun to play with friends, but you can also play it by yourself! To begin with, DO NOT look at the story on the page below. Fill in the blanks on this page with the words called for. Then, using the words you've selected, fill in the blank spaces in the story.

Now you've created your own hilarious MAD LIB!

CASPER'S LIST

ADJECTIVE: _____

ADJECTIVE: _____

NOUN: _____

NOUN: _____

NOUN: _____

PLURAL NOUN: _____

PLURAL NOUN: _____

PLURAL NOUN: _____

LIQUID: _____

PART OF BODY (PLURAL): _____

PLURAL NOUN: _____

NOUN: _____

ARTICLE OF CLOTHING:_____

CASPER'S LIST

Here is Casper's _____ list of the five _____
                   ADJECTIVE   ADJECTIVE

things that frighten a ghost the most:

1. Household appliances. A vacuum _____ , an
                                         NOUN

   automatic _____ opener, and, of course, a microwave
                      NOUN

   _____ .
      NOUN

2. Television. Especially Saturday morning _____ .
                                   PLURAL NOUN

   Most of all, ghosts are easily frightened by the 11 o'clock

   _____ .
      PLURAL NOUN

3. Ghost stories. Particularly those in which there are blood-

   curdling _____ and vampires who suck the
               PLURAL NOUN

   _____ out of human _____ .
      LIQUID   PART OF BODY (PLURAL)

4. Zippers. All ghosts are genuinely afraid of getting their white

   _____ caught in between the teeth of a
      PLURAL NOUN

   _____ .
      NOUN

5. VCR's. But then again, they frighten the _____
                                              ARTICLE OF CLOTHING

   off of everyone.

From *Casper™ MAD LIBS* ® ● Casper © 1995 UCS and Amblin, ™ Harvey
Published by Price Stern Sloan, Inc., a member of The Putnam & Grosset Group, New York, New York.

MAD LIBS® is fun to play with friends, but you can also play it by yourself! To begin with, DO NOT look at the story on the page below. Fill in the blanks on this page with the words called for. Then, using the words you've selected, fill in the blank spaces in the story.

Now you've created your own hilarious MAD LIB!

THE GHOSTLY TRIO AND CASPER

ADJECTIVE: _____

NOUN: _____

NOUN: _____

PART OF BODY: _____

PLURAL NOUN: _____

PART OF BODY: _____

NOUN: _____

ADJECTIVE: _____

PLURAL NOUN: _____

PLURAL NOUN: _____

PLURAL NOUN: _____

PART OF BODY: _____

NOUN: _____

VERB (ENDING IN "S"): _____

THE GHOSTLY TRIO AND CASPER

If it weren't for his mean and _____ uncles,
ADJECTIVE

Casper's life as a ghost would be a/an _____.
NOUN

He would be able to get up early in the _____ to go
NOUN

to school, would get to wash his _____, brush his
PART OF BODY

_____, and comb his _____.
PLURAL NOUN   PART OF BODY

Best of all, he would be able to eat all the junk _____
NOUN

he wants. Unfortunately, his _____ uncles make
ADJECTIVE

him do all the work at Whipstaff. Each day, Casper has to mess up

the _____, throw dust on the _____,
PLURAL NOUN   PLURAL NOUN

and cook all the _____. He waits on them hand and
PLURAL NOUN

_____ without ever having a _____ off
PART OF BODY   NOUN

to himself. Nevertheless, good ol' Casper _____
VERB (ENDING IN "S")

his uncles.

From *Casper*™ *MAD LIBS*® ● Casper © 1995 UCS and Amblin, ™ Harvey
Published by Price Stern Sloan, Inc., a member of The Putnam & Grosset Group, New York, New York.

MAD LIBS® is fun to play with friends, but you can also play it by yourself! To begin with, DO NOT look at the story on the page below. Fill in the blanks on this page with the words called for. Then, using the words you've selected, fill in the blank spaces in the story.

Now you've created your own hilarious MAD LIB!

TRICK OR TREATING GHOST STYLE

VERB (ENDING IN "ING"): _____

ADJECTIVE: _____

NOUN: _____

PART OF BODY: _____

NOUN: _____

ADJECTIVE: _____

PART OF BODY: _____

NOUN: _____

PART OF BODY: _____

ADJECTIVE: _____

NOUN: _____

PART OF BODY: _____

VERB (ENDING IN "S"): _____

NOUN: _____

PLURAL NOUN: _____

PLURAL NOUN: _____

TRICK OR TREATING GHOST STYLE

"I love to go trick or _____ on Halloween,"
                           VERB (ENDING IN "ING")

Kat says to Casper as they approach a dark and _____
                                                ADJECTIVE

house at the end of a long _____ .
                              NOUN

Nodding his _____ in agreement, Casper says,
                        PART OF BODY

"Halloween is my favorite _____. I love dressing up as
                                    NOUN

a/an _____ witch with a tall pointed hat on my
              ADJECTIVE

_____."
PART OF BODY

"Believe it or not," says Kat, "last year I went dressed as a ghost. I

wore a white _____, which covered my entire
                        NOUN

_____."
PART OF BODY

They reach the _____ front door of the house, but before
                     ADJECTIVE

Casper can knock, the door swings open and a huge _____
                                        NOUN

steps out and grabs Casper by his _____. Kat
                                  PART OF BODY

_____ out loud.
VERB (ENDING IN "S")

"Don't be frightened," says the owner of the house. Then he asks,

"What do you kids want, a trick or a/an _____?" Much
                                        NOUN

relieved, Kat and Casper ask for a trick. The man gives them a box

of used _____ and already-bitten, chocolate-covered
                      PLURAL NOUN

_____ .
PLURAL NOUN

From *Casper™ MAD LIBS®* ● Casper © 1995 UCS and Amblin, ™ Harvey
Published by Price Stern Sloan, Inc., a member of The Putnam & Grosset Group, New York, New York.